MW00639865

My #BookTok Reading Journal

TRACK & REVIEW
YOUR FAVORITE READS

CASTLE POINT BOOKS
NEW YORK

This journal belongs to:

_____

How to Use This Journal

ONLY BOOKTOK UNDERSTANDS the beauty of ugly crying into a pillow (or your snuggly pet cat) on a lazy Sunday morning as you process the heart-stopping conclusion of a new favorite novel.

My #BookTok Reading Journal will help you track and review the memorable books you meet on your BookTok journey, especially the ones that you can't stand to put down. From spicy romance to thrilling suspense, books are like relationships—you never know which one will be your soulmate.

Keep this adorable journal on your nightstand and fill it with your personal thoughts. You fell in love with the villain? You flipped ahead to the bedroom scene? Spill the tea. Jot down the thoughts and emotions and opinions that bubble to the surface as you work your way through that growing TBR pile.

With *My #BookTok Reading Journal*, you can just be unapologetically you. Whether you're fueled by fantasy, inspired by literature, or hot for romance, you are part of the bold TikTok revolution of readers whose nights and weekends are almost always fully booked. 😊

I ♡ BOOKTOK

BookTok never fails to...

My favorite BookTokers are...

My favorite authors are...

The kind of books I like are...

BookTok challenges I've tried / want to try...

Reading Goals

Create some reading resolutions below. See how many books you can read in a week, a month, or even a year! Add a date and put it in your phone to remind yourself of your goal.

_____ by [/ /]

_____ by [/ /]

_____ by [/ /]

_____ by [/ /]

_____ by [/ /]

MY TBR LIST

_____   _____

_____   _____

_____   _____

_____   _____

_____   _____

_____   _____

_____   _____

BOOK TITLE: The lost Bookshop

AUTHOR:

My review:

_____

_____

_____

_____

_____

_____

My favorite part/quote:

_____

_____

_____

_____

My favorite character:

Henry

Someone I know who would love this book:

Thanks Jackie for the recom

Star rating:	Tears shed:	Spice meter:
☆☆☆☆☆	◊◊◊◊◊	🍌🍌🍌🍌🍌

BOOK TITLE: The fine print
AUTHOR:

My review:

_____

_____

_____

_____

_____

_____

My favorite part/quote:

_____

_____

_____

_____

My favorite character:

_____

Someone I know who would love this book:

_____

Star rating:	Tears shed:	Spice meter:
☆☆☆☆☆	◇◇◇◇◇◇	🌶🌶🌶🌶🌶

BOOK TITLE: Heartstopper volume 5
AUTHOR: Alice Oseman

My review:

_____
_____
_____
_____
_____
_____

My favorite part/quote:

_____
_____
_____
_____

My favorite character:
Nick and charlie

Someone I know who would love this book:

_____

Star rating:	Tears shed:	Spice meter:
★★★★☆	◊ ◊ ◊ ◊ ◊	🌶🌶🌶🌶🌶

BOOK TITLE:
AUTHOR:

My review:

_____

_____

_____

_____

_____

_____

My favorite part/quote:

_____

_____

_____

_____

My favorite character:

_____

Someone I know who would love this book:

_____

Star rating:	Tears shed:	Spice meter:
☆☆☆☆☆	◇◇◇◇◇	🌶🌶🌶🌶🌶

BOOK TITLE:
AUTHOR:

My review:

_____
_____
_____
_____
_____
_____

My favorite part/quote:

_____
_____
_____
_____

My favorite character:

_____

Someone I know who would love this book:

_____

Star rating:	Tears shed:	Spice meter:
☆ ☆ ☆ ☆ ☆	◊ ◊ ◊ ◊ ◊	🌶 🌶 🌶 🌶 🌶

BOOK TITLE:
AUTHOR:

My review:

_____
_____
_____
_____
_____
_____

My favorite part/quote:

_____
_____
_____
_____

My favorite character:

_____

Someone I know who would love this book:

_____

| Star rating: | Tears shed: | Spice meter: |
| ☆ ☆ ☆ ☆ ☆ | ◊ ◊ ◊ ◊ ◊ | 🌶 🌶 🌶 🌶 🌶 |

BOOK TITLE:
AUTHOR:

My review:

_____
_____
_____
_____
_____
_____

My favorite part/quote:

_____
_____
_____
_____

My favorite character:

_____

Someone I know who would love this book:

_____

Star rating:	Tears shed:	Spice meter:
☆☆☆☆☆	⬠⬠⬠⬠⬠	🌶🌶🌶🌶🌶

BOOK TITLE:
AUTHOR:

My review:

_____

_____

_____

_____

_____

_____

My favorite part/quote:

_____

_____

_____

_____

My favorite character:

_____

Someone I know who would love this book:

_____

| Star rating: | Tears shed: | Spice meter: |
| ☆ ☆ ☆ ☆ ☆ | ◌ ◌ ◌ ◌ ◌ | 🌶 🌶 🌶 🌶 🌶 |

BOOK TITLE:
AUTHOR:

My review:

_____
_____
_____
_____
_____
_____

My favorite part/quote:

_____
_____
_____
_____

My favorite character:

_____

Someone I know who would love this book:

_____

| Star rating: | Tears shed: | Spice meter: |
| ☆☆☆☆☆ | ◇◇◇◇◇ | 🌶🌶🌶🌶🌶 |

BOOK TITLE:
AUTHOR:

My review:

_____

_____

_____

_____

_____

_____

My favorite part/quote:

_____

_____

_____

_____

My favorite character:

_____

Someone I know who would love this book:

_____

| *Star rating:* | *Tears shed:* | *Spice meter:* |
| ☆☆☆☆☆ | ◌ ◌ ◌ ◌ ◌ | 🌶 🌶 🌶 🌶 🌶 |

BOOK TITLE:
AUTHOR:

My review:

_____
_____
_____
_____
_____
_____

My favorite part/quote:

_____
_____
_____
_____

My favorite character:

_____

Someone I know who would love this book:

_____

Star rating:	Tears shed:	Spice meter:
☆☆☆☆☆	◊◊◊◊◊	🌶🌶🌶🌶🌶

BOOK TITLE:
AUTHOR:

My review:

_____
_____
_____
_____
_____
_____

My favorite part/quote:

_____
_____
_____
_____

My favorite character:

_____

Someone I know who would love this book:

_____

Star rating:
☆ ☆ ☆ ☆ ☆

Tears shed:
◌ ◌ ◌ ◌ ◌

Spice meter:
🌶 🌶 🌶 🌶 🌶

BOOK TITLE:
AUTHOR:

My review:

_____
_____
_____
_____
_____
_____

My favorite part/quote:

_____
_____
_____
_____

My favorite character:

_____

Someone I know who would love this book:

_____

Star rating:	Tears shed:	Spice meter:
☆☆☆☆☆	◊◊◊◊◊	🌶🌶🌶🌶🌶

BOOK TITLE:
AUTHOR:

My review:

_____

_____

_____

_____

_____

_____

My favorite part/quote:

_____

_____

_____

_____

My favorite character:

_____

Someone I know who would love this book:

_____

Star rating:
☆ ☆ ☆ ☆ ☆

Tears shed:
◊ ◊ ◊ ◊ ◊

Spice meter:
🌶 🌶 🌶 🌶 🌶

BOOK TITLE:
AUTHOR:

My review:

_____
_____
_____
_____
_____
_____

My favorite part/quote:

_____
_____
_____
_____

My favorite character:

_____

Someone I know who would love this book:

_____

Star rating:	Tears shed:	Spice meter:
☆☆☆☆☆	◊◊◊◊◊	🌶🌶🌶🌶🌶

BOOK TITLE:
AUTHOR:

My review:

_____
_____
_____
_____
_____
_____

My favorite part/quote:

_____
_____
_____
_____

My favorite character:

_____

Someone I know who would love this book:

_____

Star rating:
☆ ☆ ☆ ☆ ☆

Tears shed:
◊ ◊ ◊ ◊ ◊

Spice meter:

BOOK TITLE:
AUTHOR:

My review:

_____
_____
_____
_____
_____
_____

My favorite part/quote:

_____
_____
_____
_____

My favorite character:

_____

Someone I know who would love this book:

_____

Star rating:	Tears shed:	Spice meter:
☆☆☆☆☆	◌◌◌◌◌	🌶🌶🌶🌶🌶

BOOK TITLE:
AUTHOR:

My review:

_____
_____
_____
_____
_____
_____

My favorite part/quote:

_____
_____
_____
_____

My favorite character:

_____

Someone I know who would love this book:

_____

Star rating:	Tears shed:	Spice meter:
☆☆☆☆☆	◇◇◇◇◇	🌶🌶🌶🌶🌶

BOOK TITLE:
AUTHOR:

My review:

_____
_____
_____
_____
_____
_____

My favorite part/quote:

_____
_____
_____
_____

My favorite character:

_____

Someone I know who would love this book:

_____

Star rating:	Tears shed:	Spice meter:
☆ ☆ ☆ ☆ ☆	○ ○ ○ ○ ○	🌶 🌶 🌶 🌶 🌶

BOOK TITLE:
AUTHOR:

My review:

_____

_____

_____

_____

_____

_____

My favorite part/quote:

_____

_____

_____

_____

My favorite character:

_____

Someone I know who would love this book:

_____

Star rating:	Tears shed:	Spice meter:
☆ ☆ ☆ ☆ ☆	◌ ◌ ◌ ◌ ◌	🌶 🌶 🌶 🌶 🌶

BOOK TITLE:
AUTHOR:

My review:

My favorite part/quote:

My favorite character:

Someone I know who would love this book:

Star rating:
☆☆☆☆☆

Tears shed:
◇ ◇ ◇ ◇ ◇

Spice meter:
🌶 🌶 🌶 🌶 🌶

BOOK TITLE:
AUTHOR:

My review:

_____

_____

_____

_____

_____

_____

My favorite part/quote:

_____

_____

_____

_____

My favorite character:

_____

Someone I know who would love this book:

_____

Star rating:	Tears shed:	Spice meter:
☆ ☆ ☆ ☆ ☆	◊ ◊ ◊ ◊ ◊	🌶 🌶 🌶 🌶 🌶

BOOK TITLE:
AUTHOR:

My review:

_____
_____
_____
_____
_____
_____

My favorite part/quote:

_____
_____
_____
_____

My favorite character:

_____

Someone I know who would love this book:

_____

Star rating:	Tears shed:	Spice meter:
☆☆☆☆☆	◌◌◌◌◌	🌶🌶🌶🌶🌶

BOOK TITLE:
AUTHOR:

My review:

_____
_____
_____
_____
_____
_____

My favorite part/quote:

_____
_____
_____

My favorite character:

_____

Someone I know who would love this book:

_____

Star rating:	Tears shed:	Spice meter:
☆☆☆☆☆	◇◇◇◇◇	🌶🌶🌶🌶🌶

BOOK TITLE:
AUTHOR:

My review:

_____
_____
_____
_____
_____
_____

My favorite part/quote:

_____
_____
_____
_____

My favorite character:

_____

Someone I know who would love this book:

_____

Star rating:	Tears shed:	Spice meter:
☆☆☆☆☆	◊◊◊◊◊	🌶🌶🌶🌶🌶

BOOK TITLE:
AUTHOR:

My review:

_____

_____

_____

_____

_____

My favorite part/quote:

_____

_____

_____

My favorite character:

_____

Someone I know who would love this book:

_____

Star rating:
☆ ☆ ☆ ☆ ☆

Tears shed:
◊ ◊ ◊ ◊ ◊

Spice meter:
🌶 🌶 🌶 🌶 🌶

BOOK TITLE:
AUTHOR:

My review:

_____
_____
_____
_____
_____
_____

My favorite part/quote:

_____
_____
_____
_____

My favorite character:

_____

Someone I know who would love this book:

_____

Star rating:	Tears shed:	Spice meter:
☆ ☆ ☆ ☆ ☆	◊ ◊ ◊ ◊ ◊	🌶 🌶 🌶 🌶 🌶

BOOK TITLE:
AUTHOR:

My review:

_____

_____

_____

_____

_____

_____

My favorite part/quote:

_____

_____

_____

My favorite character:

_____

Someone I know who would love this book:

_____

| Star rating: | Tears shed: | Spice meter: |
| ☆ ☆ ☆ ☆ ☆ | ◊ ◊ ◊ ◊ ◊ | 🌶 🌶 🌶 🌶 🌶 |

BOOK TITLE:
AUTHOR:

My review:

My favorite part/quote:

My favorite character:

Someone I know who would love this book:

Star rating:	Tears shed:	Spice meter:
☆☆☆☆☆	◊◊◊◊◊	🌶🌶🌶🌶🌶

BOOK TITLE:
AUTHOR:

My review:

_____
_____
_____
_____
_____
_____

My favorite part/quote:

_____
_____
_____
_____

My favorite character:

_____

Someone I know who would love this book:

_____

| Star rating: | Tears shed: | Spice meter: |
| ☆ ☆ ☆ ☆ ☆ | ◇ ◇ ◇ ◇ ◇ | 🌶 🌶 🌶 🌶 🌶 |

BOOK TITLE:
AUTHOR:

My review:

_____
_____
_____
_____
_____
_____

My favorite part/quote:

_____
_____
_____

My favorite character:

_____

Someone I know who would love this book:

_____

| Star rating: | Tears shed: | Spice meter: |
| ☆ ☆ ☆ ☆ ☆ | ◊ ◊ ◊ ◊ ◊ | 🌶 🌶 🌶 🌶 🌶 |

BOOK TITLE:
AUTHOR:

My review:

_____

_____

_____

_____

_____

_____

My favorite part/quote:

_____

_____

_____

_____

My favorite character:

_____

Someone I know who would love this book:

_____

Star rating:	Tears shed:	Spice meter:
☆☆☆☆☆	◇◇◇◇◇	🌶🌶🌶🌶🌶

BOOK TITLE:
AUTHOR:

My review:

My favorite part/quote:

My favorite character:

Someone I know who would love this book:

Star rating:
☆☆☆☆☆

Tears shed:
◌ ◌ ◌ ◌ ◌

Spice meter:
🌶 🌶 🌶 🌶 🌶

BOOK TITLE:
AUTHOR:

My review:

_____

_____

_____

_____

_____

_____

My favorite part/quote:

_____

_____

_____

_____

My favorite character:

_____

Someone I know who would love this book:

_____

Star rating:	_Tears shed:_	_Spice meter:_
☆ ☆ ☆ ☆ ☆	◊ ◊ ◊ ◊ ◊	🌶 🌶 🌶 🌶 🌶

BOOK TITLE:
AUTHOR:

My review:

_____

_____

_____

_____

_____

_____

My favorite part/quote:

_____

_____

_____

_____

My favorite character:

_____

Someone I know who would love this book:

_____

Star rating:	*Tears shed:*	*Spice meter:*
☆ ☆ ☆ ☆ ☆	◊ ◊ ◊ ◊ ◊	🌶 🌶 🌶 🌶 🌶

BOOK TITLE:
AUTHOR:

My review:

_____
_____
_____
_____
_____
_____

My favorite part/quote:

_____
_____
_____
_____

My favorite character:

_____

Someone I know who would love this book:

_____

Star rating:	_Tears shed:_	_Spice meter:_
☆ ☆ ☆ ☆ ☆	◊ ◊ ◊ ◊ ◊	

BOOK TITLE:
AUTHOR:

My review:

My favorite part/quote:

My favorite character:

Someone I know who would love this book:

Star rating:	Tears shed:	Spice meter:
☆ ☆ ☆ ☆ ☆	◊ ◊ ◊ ◊ ◊	🌶 🌶 🌶 🌶 🌶

BOOK TITLE:
AUTHOR:

My review:

_____

_____

_____

_____

_____

_____

My favorite part/quote:

_____

_____

_____

_____

My favorite character:

_____

Someone I know who would love this book:

_____

Star rating:
☆ ☆ ☆ ☆ ☆

Tears shed:
◊ ◊ ◊ ◊ ◊

Spice meter:
🌶 🌶 🌶 🌶 🌶

BOOK TITLE:
AUTHOR:

My review:

_____
_____
_____
_____
_____

My favorite part/quote:

_____
_____
_____
_____

My favorite character:

_____

Someone I know who would love this book:

_____

Star rating:	Tears shed:	Spice meter:
☆☆☆☆☆	◊◊◊◊◊	🌶🌶🌶🌶🌶

BOOK TITLE:
AUTHOR:

My review:

_____

_____

_____

_____

_____

_____

My favorite part/quote:

_____

_____

_____

_____

My favorite character:

_____

Someone I know who would love this book:

_____

| _Star rating:_ | _Tears shed:_ | _Spice meter:_ |
| ☆☆☆☆☆ | ◌◌◌◌◌ | 🌶🌶🌶🌶🌶 |

BOOK TITLE:
AUTHOR:

My review:

My favorite part/quote:

My favorite character:

Someone I know who would love this book:

Star rating:	Tears shed:	Spice meter:
☆☆☆☆☆	◊◊◊◊◊	🌶🌶🌶🌶🌶

BOOK TITLE:
AUTHOR:

My review:

_____
_____
_____
_____
_____
_____

My favorite part/quote:

_____
_____
_____
_____

My favorite character:

_____

Someone I know who would love this book:

_____

Star rating:	*Tears shed:*	*Spice meter:*
☆☆☆☆☆	◊◊◊◊◊	🌶🌶🌶🌶🌶

BOOK TITLE:
AUTHOR:

My review:

My favorite part/quote:

My favorite character:

Someone I know who would love this book:

Star rating:
☆ ☆ ☆ ☆ ☆

Tears shed:
◊ ◊ ◊ ◊ ◊

Spice meter:
🌶 🌶 🌶 🌶 🌶

BOOK TITLE:
AUTHOR:

My review:

_____

_____

_____

_____

_____

_____

My favorite part/quote:

_____

_____

_____

_____

My favorite character:

_____

Someone I know who would love this book:

_____

Star rating:
☆☆☆☆☆

Tears shed:
◊ ◊ ◊ ◊ ◊

Spice meter:
🌶 🌶 🌶 🌶 🌶

BOOK TITLE:
AUTHOR:

My review:

_____
_____
_____
_____
_____
_____

My favorite part/quote:

_____
_____
_____
_____

My favorite character:

_____

Someone I know who would love this book:

_____

Star rating:
☆ ☆ ☆ ☆ ☆

Tears shed:
◇ ◇ ◇ ◇ ◇

Spice meter:
🌶 🌶 🌶 🌶 🌶

My review:

_____

_____

_____

_____

_____

_____

My favorite part/quote:

_____

_____

_____

_____

My favorite character:

_____

Someone I know who would love this book:

_____

Star rating:	Tears shed:	Spice meter:
☆ ☆ ☆ ☆ ☆	◇ ◇ ◇ ◇ ◇	🌶 🌶 🌶 🌶 🌶

BOOK TITLE:
AUTHOR:

My review:

My favorite part/quote:

My favorite character:

Someone I know who would love this book:

Star rating:	Tears shed:	Spice meter:
☆☆☆☆☆	◊◊◊◊◊	🌶🌶🌶🌶🌶

BOOK TITLE:
AUTHOR:

My review:

_____

_____

_____

_____

_____

_____

My favorite part/quote:

_____

_____

_____

_____

My favorite character:

_____

Someone I know who would love this book:

_____

| Star rating: | Tears shed: | Spice meter: |
| ☆ ☆ ☆ ☆ ☆ | ◊ ◊ ◊ ◊ ◊ | 🌶 🌶 🌶 🌶 🌶 |

BOOK TITLE:
AUTHOR:

My review:

My favorite part/quote:

My favorite character:

Someone I know who would love this book:

Star rating:	Tears shed:	Spice meter:
☆☆☆☆☆	◊◊◊◊◊	🌶🌶🌶🌶🌶

BOOK TITLE:
AUTHOR:

My review:

_____

_____

_____

_____

_____

_____

My favorite part/quote:

_____

_____

_____

My favorite character:

_____

Someone I know who would love this book:

_____

Star rating:	Tears shed:	Spice meter:
☆☆☆☆☆	◇◇◇◇◇	🌶🌶🌶🌶🌶

BOOK TITLE:
AUTHOR:

My review:

My favorite part/quote:

My favorite character:

Someone I know who would love this book:

| Star rating: | Tears shed: | Spice meter: |
| ☆☆☆☆☆ | ◊◊◊◊◊ | 🌶🌶🌶🌶🌶 |

BOOK TITLE:
AUTHOR:

My review:

_____

_____

_____

_____

_____

_____

My favorite part/quote:

_____

_____

_____

_____

My favorite character:

_____

Someone I know who would love this book:

_____

| Star rating: | Tears shed: | Spice meter: |
| ☆☆☆☆☆ | ◇◇◇◇◇ | 🌶🌶🌶🌶🌶 |

BOOK TITLE:
AUTHOR:

My review:

My favorite part/quote:

My favorite character:

Someone I know who would love this book:

Star rating:	Tears shed:	Spice meter:
☆ ☆ ☆ ☆ ☆	◇ ◇ ◇ ◇ ◇	🌶 🌶 🌶 🌶 🌶

BOOK TITLE:
AUTHOR:

My review:

_____

_____

_____

_____

_____

_____

My favorite part/quote:

_____

_____

_____

My favorite character:

_____

Someone I know who would love this book:

_____

Star rating:	Tears shed:	Spice meter:
☆ ☆ ☆ ☆ ☆	◊ ◊ ◊ ◊ ◊	🌶 🌶 🌶 🌶 🌶

BOOK TITLE:
AUTHOR:

My review:

My favorite part/quote:

My favorite character:

Someone I know who would love this book:

Star rating:	Tears shed:	Spice meter:
☆☆☆☆☆	◊◊◊◊◊	🌶🌶🌶🌶🌶

BOOK TITLE:
AUTHOR:

My review:

_____

_____

_____

_____

_____

_____

My favorite part/quote:

_____

_____

_____

My favorite character:

_____

Someone I know who would love this book:

_____

Star rating:	Tears shed:	Spice meter:
☆ ☆ ☆ ☆ ☆	◌ ◌ ◌ ◌ ◌	🌶 🌶 🌶 🌶 🌶

BOOK TITLE:
AUTHOR:

My review:

_____

_____

_____

_____

_____

My favorite part/quote:

_____

_____

_____

My favorite character:

_____

Someone I know who would love this book:

_____

| Star rating: | Tears shed: | Spice meter: |
| ☆ ☆ ☆ ☆ ☆ | ◇ ◇ ◇ ◇ ◇ | 🌶 🌶 🌶 🌶 🌶 |

BOOK TITLE:
AUTHOR:

My review:

_____

_____

_____

_____

_____

My favorite part/quote:

_____

_____

_____

My favorite character:

_____

Someone I know who would love this book:

_____

| _Star rating:_ | _Tears shed:_ | _Spice meter:_ |
| ☆☆☆☆☆ | ◊◊◊◊◊ | 🌶🌶🌶🌶🌶 |

BOOK TITLE:
AUTHOR:

My review:

_____

_____

_____

_____

_____

_____

My favorite part/quote:

_____

_____

_____

_____

My favorite character:

_____

Someone I know who would love this book:

_____

| Star rating: | Tears shed: | Spice meter: |
| ☆ ☆ ☆ ☆ ☆ | ◊ ◊ ◊ ◊ ◊ | 🌶 🌶 🌶 🌶 🌶 |

BOOK TITLE:
AUTHOR:

My review:

_____
_____
_____
_____
_____
_____

My favorite part/quote:

_____
_____
_____
_____

My favorite character:

_____

Someone I know who would love this book:

_____

| Star rating: | Tears shed: | Spice meter: |
| ☆☆☆☆☆ | ◇◇◇◇◇ | 🌶🌶🌶🌶🌶 |

BOOK TITLE:
AUTHOR:

My review:

My favorite part/quote:

My favorite character:

Someone I know who would love this book:

 Star rating: 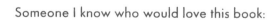 Tears shed: Spice meter:
☆ ☆ ☆ ☆ ☆   ◊ ◊ ◊ ◊ ◊

BOOK TITLE:
AUTHOR:

My review:

_____
_____
_____
_____
_____
_____

My favorite part/quote:

_____
_____
_____
_____

My favorite character:

_____

Someone I know who would love this book:

_____

| Star rating: | Tears shed: | Spice meter: |
| ☆ ☆ ☆ ☆ ☆ | ◌ ◌ ◌ ◌ ◌ | 🌶 🌶 🌶 🌶 🌶 |

BOOK TITLE:
AUTHOR:

My review:

_____

_____

_____

_____

_____

_____

My favorite part/quote:

_____

_____

_____

My favorite character:

_____

Someone I know who would love this book:

_____

Star rating:	Tears shed:	Spice meter:
☆☆☆☆☆	◊◊◊◊◊	🌶🌶🌶🌶🌶

BOOK TITLE:
AUTHOR:

My review:

_____
_____
_____
_____
_____
_____

My favorite part/quote:

_____
_____
_____

My favorite character:

_____

Someone I know who would love this book:

_____

| Star rating: | Tears shed: | Spice meter: |
| ☆ ☆ ☆ ☆ ☆ | ◌ ◌ ◌ ◌ ◌ | 🌶 🌶 🌶 🌶 🌶 |

BOOK TITLE:
AUTHOR:

My review:

_____

_____

_____

_____

_____

My favorite part/quote:

_____

_____

_____

My favorite character:

_____

Someone I know who would love this book:

_____

| Star rating: | Tears shed: | Spice meter: |
| ☆ ☆ ☆ ☆ ☆ | ◌ ◌ ◌ ◌ ◌ | 🌶 🌶 🌶 🌶 🌶 |

BOOK TITLE:
AUTHOR:

My review:

_____

_____

_____

_____

_____

_____

My favorite part/quote:

_____

_____

_____

_____

My favorite character:

_____

Someone I know who would love this book:

_____

Star rating:	Tears shed:	Spice meter:
☆☆☆☆☆	◊◊◊◊◊	🌶🌶🌶🌶🌶

BOOK TITLE:
AUTHOR:

My review:

_____
_____
_____
_____
_____
_____

My favorite part/quote:

_____
_____
_____
_____

My favorite character:

_____

Someone I know who would love this book:

_____

| Star rating: | Tears shed: | Spice meter: |
| ☆ ☆ ☆ ☆ ☆ | ◊ ◊ ◊ ◊ ◊ | 🌶 🌶 🌶 🌶 🌶 |

BOOK TITLE:
AUTHOR:

My review:

_____

_____

_____

_____

_____

_____

My favorite part/quote:

_____

_____

_____

_____

My favorite character:

_____

Someone I know who would love this book:

_____

Star rating:	Tears shed:	Spice meter:
☆ ☆ ☆ ☆ ☆	◊ ◊ ◊ ◊ ◊	🌶 🌶 🌶 🌶 🌶

BOOK TITLE:
AUTHOR:

My review:

My favorite part/quote:

My favorite character:

Someone I know who would love this book:

Star rating:	Tears shed:	Spice meter:
☆ ☆ ☆ ☆ ☆	◌ ◌ ◌ ◌ ◌	🌶 🌶 🌶 🌶 🌶

BOOK TITLE:
AUTHOR:

My review:

_____
_____
_____
_____
_____

My favorite part/quote:

_____
_____
_____
_____

My favorite character:

_____

Someone I know who would love this book:

_____

Star rating: Tears shed: Spice meter:
☆ ☆ ☆ ☆ ☆   ◌ ◌ ◌ ◌ ◌   🌶 🌶 🌶 🌶 🌶

BOOK TITLE:
AUTHOR:

My review:

_____
_____
_____
_____
_____
_____

My favorite part/quote:

_____
_____
_____
_____

My favorite character:

_____

Someone I know who would love this book:

_____

Star rating:	Tears shed:	Spice meter:
☆☆☆☆☆	◇◇◇◇◇	🌶🌶🌶🌶🌶

BOOK TITLE:
AUTHOR:

My review:

_____

_____

_____

_____

_____

_____

My favorite part/quote:

_____

_____

_____

_____

My favorite character:

_____

Someone I know who would love this book:

_____

| Star rating: | Tears shed: | Spice meter: |
| ☆☆☆☆☆ | ○ ○ ○ ○ ○ | 🌶 🌶 🌶 🌶 🌶 |

BOOK TITLE:
AUTHOR:

My review:

My favorite part/quote:

My favorite character:

Someone I know who would love this book:

Star rating:	Tears shed:	Spice meter:
☆ ☆ ☆ ☆ ☆	◊ ◊ ◊ ◊ ◊	🌶 🌶 🌶 🌶 🌶

My review:

_____

_____

_____

_____

_____

_____

My favorite part/quote:

_____

_____

_____

_____

My favorite character:

_____

Someone I know who would love this book:

_____

Star rating:	Tears shed:	Spice meter:
☆☆☆☆☆	◊ ◊ ◊ ◊ ◊	🌶 🌶 🌶 🌶 🌶

BOOK TITLE:
AUTHOR:

My review:

_____
_____
_____
_____
_____
_____

My favorite part/quote:

_____
_____
_____
_____

My favorite character:

_____

Someone I know who would love this book:

_____

Star rating:	Tears shed:	Spice meter:
☆ ☆ ☆ ☆ ☆	◌ ◌ ◌ ◌ ◌	🌶 🌶 🌶 🌶 🌶

BOOK TITLE:
AUTHOR:

My review:

_____

_____

_____

_____

_____

_____

My favorite part/quote:

_____

_____

_____

_____

My favorite character:

_____

Someone I know who would love this book:

_____

Star rating:	*Tears shed:*	*Spice meter:*

BOOK TITLE:
AUTHOR:

My review:

My favorite part/quote:

My favorite character:

Someone I know who would love this book:

Star rating:
☆ ☆ ☆ ☆ ☆

Tears shed:
◊ ◊ ◊ ◊ ◊

Spice meter:
🌶 🌶 🌶 🌶 🌶

BOOK TITLE:
AUTHOR:

My review:

_____
_____
_____
_____
_____

My favorite part/quote:

_____
_____
_____
_____

My favorite character:

_____

Someone I know who would love this book:

_____

Star rating:	Tears shed:	Spice meter:
☆ ☆ ☆ ☆ ☆	◌ ◌ ◌ ◌ ◌	🌶 🌶 🌶 🌶 🌶

BOOK TITLE:
AUTHOR:

My review:

_____
_____
_____
_____
_____
_____

My favorite part/quote:

_____
_____
_____
_____

My favorite character:

_____

Someone I know who would love this book:

_____

Star rating:	Tears shed:	Spice meter:
☆☆☆☆☆	◊ ◊ ◊ ◊ ◊	🌶🌶🌶🌶🌶

My review:

_____
_____
_____
_____
_____
_____

My favorite part/quote:

_____
_____
_____
_____

My favorite character:

_____

Someone I know who would love this book:

_____

Star rating:	*Tears shed:*	*Spice meter:*
☆ ☆ ☆ ☆ ☆	◊ ◊ ◊ ◊ ◊	🌶 🌶 🌶 🌶 🌶

BOOK TITLE:
AUTHOR:

My review:

_____
_____
_____
_____
_____
_____

My favorite part/quote:

_____
_____
_____
_____

My favorite character:

_____

Someone I know who would love this book:

_____

| Star rating: | Tears shed: | Spice meter: |
| ☆ ☆ ☆ ☆ ☆ | ◇ ◇ ◇ ◇ ◇ | 🌶 🌶 🌶 🌶 🌶 |

BOOK TITLE:
AUTHOR:

My review:

_____

_____

_____

_____

_____

_____

My favorite part/quote:

_____

_____

_____

My favorite character:

_____

Someone I know who would love this book:

_____

| Star rating: | Tears shed: | Spice meter: |
| ☆☆☆☆☆ | ◇◇◇◇◇ | 🌶🌶🌶🌶🌶 |

BOOK TITLE:
AUTHOR:

My review:

_____
_____
_____
_____
_____
_____

My favorite part/quote:

_____
_____
_____
_____

My favorite character:

_____

Someone I know who would love this book:

_____

| Star rating: | Tears shed: | Spice meter: |
| ☆☆☆☆☆ | ◊◊◊◊◊ | 🌶🌶🌶🌶🌶 |

BOOK TITLE:
AUTHOR:

My review:

_____

_____

_____

_____

_____

_____

My favorite part/quote:

_____

_____

_____

_____

My favorite character:

_____

Someone I know who would love this book:

_____

Star rating:	Tears shed:	Spice meter:
☆ ☆ ☆ ☆ ☆	◊ ◊ ◊ ◊ ◊	🌶 🌶 🌶 🌶 🌶

BOOK TITLE:
AUTHOR:

My review:

_____

_____

_____

_____

_____

_____

My favorite part/quote:

_____

_____

_____

_____

My favorite character:

_____

Someone I know who would love this book:

_____

Star rating:	Tears shed:	Spice meter:
☆ ☆ ☆ ☆ ☆	◊ ◊ ◊ ◊ ◊	🌶 🌶 🌶 🌶 🌶

BOOK TITLE:
AUTHOR:

My review:

_____

_____

_____

_____

_____

_____

My favorite part/quote:

_____

_____

_____

My favorite character:

_____

Someone I know who would love this book:

_____

Star rating:	Tears shed:	Spice meter:
☆ ☆ ☆ ☆ ☆	◊ ◊ ◊ ◊ ◊	🌶 🌶 🌶 🌶 🌶

BOOK TITLE:
AUTHOR:

My review:

My favorite part/quote:

My favorite character:

Someone I know who would love this book:

Star rating:	Tears shed:	Spice meter:
☆ ☆ ☆ ☆ ☆	〇 〇 〇 〇 〇	🌶 🌶 🌶 🌶 🌶

BOOK TITLE:
AUTHOR:

My review:

_____
_____
_____
_____
_____
_____

My favorite part/quote:

_____
_____
_____
_____

My favorite character:

_____

Someone I know who would love this book:

_____

Star rating: Tears shed: Spice meter:
☆ ☆ ☆ ☆ ☆   ◇ ◇ ◇ ◇ ◇   🌶 🌶 🌶 🌶 🌶

BOOK TITLE:
AUTHOR:

My review:

My favorite part/quote:

My favorite character:

Someone I know who would love this book:

Star rating:
☆ ☆ ☆ ☆ ☆

Tears shed:

Spice meter:

BOOK TITLE:
AUTHOR:

My review:

_____
_____
_____
_____
_____
_____

My favorite part/quote:

_____
_____
_____

My favorite character:

_____

Someone I know who would love this book:

_____

Star rating:	Tears shed:	Spice meter:
☆☆☆☆☆	◊◊◊◊◊	🌶🌶🌶🌶🌶

BOOK TITLE:
AUTHOR:

My review:

My favorite part/quote:

My favorite character:

Someone I know who would love this book:

Star rating:	Tears shed:	Spice meter:
☆ ☆ ☆ ☆ ☆	◊ ◊ ◊ ◊ ◊	⌇ ⌇ ⌇ ⌇ ⌇

BOOK TITLE:
AUTHOR:

My review:

_____

_____

_____

_____

_____

_____

My favorite part/quote:

_____

_____

_____

_____

My favorite character:

_____

Someone I know who would love this book:

_____

Star rating:	Tears shed:	Spice meter:
☆ ☆ ☆ ☆ ☆	◊ ◊ ◊ ◊ ◊	🌶 🌶 🌶 🌶 🌶

BOOK TITLE:
AUTHOR:

My review:

_____
_____
_____
_____
_____
_____

My favorite part/quote:

_____
_____
_____
_____

My favorite character:

_____

Someone I know who would love this book:

_____

| Star rating: | Tears shed: | Spice meter: |
| ☆ ☆ ☆ ☆ ☆ | ◊ ◊ ◊ ◊ ◊ | 🌶 🌶 🌶 🌶 🌶 |

BOOK TITLE:
AUTHOR:

My review:

My favorite part/quote:

My favorite character:

Someone I know who would love this book:

Star rating:	Tears shed:	Spice meter:
☆☆☆☆☆	◊◊◊◊◊	🌶🌶🌶🌶🌶

BOOK TITLE:
AUTHOR:

My review:

My favorite part/quote:

My favorite character:

Someone I know who would love this book:

Star rating:	Tears shed:	Spice meter:
☆ ☆ ☆ ☆ ☆	◊ ◊ ◊ ◊ ◊	🌶 🌶 🌶 🌶 🌶

BOOK TITLE:
AUTHOR:

My review:

_____
_____
_____
_____
_____
_____

My favorite part/quote:

_____
_____
_____
_____

My favorite character:

_____

Someone I know who would love this book:

_____

| Star rating: | Tears shed: | Spice meter: |
| ☆☆☆☆☆ | ◊ ◊ ◊ ◊ ◊ | 🌶 🌶 🌶 🌶 🌶 |

BOOK TITLE:
AUTHOR:

My review:

_____

_____

_____

_____

_____

My favorite part/quote:

_____

_____

_____

_____

My favorite character:

_____

Someone I know who would love this book:

_____

Star rating:	Tears shed:	Spice meter:
☆ ☆ ☆ ☆ ☆	◊ ◊ ◊ ◊ ◊	🌶 🌶 🌶 🌶 🌶

BOOK TITLE:
AUTHOR:

My review:

_____

_____

_____

_____

_____

_____

My favorite part/quote:

_____

_____

_____

_____

My favorite character:

_____

Someone I know who would love this book:

_____

Star rating:	Tears shed:	Spice meter:
☆ ☆ ☆ ☆ ☆	◇ ◇ ◇ ◇ ◇	🌶 🌶 🌶 🌶 🌶

BOOK TITLE:
AUTHOR:

My review:

My favorite part/quote:

My favorite character:

Someone I know who would love this book:

Star rating:	Tears shed:	Spice meter:
☆ ☆ ☆ ☆ ☆	◊ ◊ ◊ ◊ ◊	🌶 🌶 🌶 🌶 🌶

BOOK TITLE:
AUTHOR:

My review:

My favorite part/quote:

My favorite character:

Someone I know who would love this book:

Star rating:	Tears shed:	Spice meter:
☆ ☆ ☆ ☆ ☆	◊ ◊ ◊ ◊ ◊	🌶 🌶 🌶 🌶 🌶

BOOK TITLE:
AUTHOR:

My review:

_____
_____
_____
_____
_____

My favorite part/quote:

_____
_____
_____
_____

My favorite character:

_____

Someone I know who would love this book:

_____

| *Star rating:* | *Tears shed:* | *Spice meter:* |
| ☆☆☆☆☆ | ◊◊◊◊◊ | 🌶🌶🌶🌶🌶 |

BOOK TITLE:
AUTHOR:

My review:

_____

_____

_____

_____

_____

_____

My favorite part/quote:

_____

_____

_____

_____

My favorite character:

_____

Someone I know who would love this book:

_____

Star rating:
☆ ☆ ☆ ☆ ☆

Tears shed:
◇ ◇ ◇ ◇ ◇

Spice meter:
🌶 🌶 🌶 🌶 🌶

BOOK TITLE:
AUTHOR:

My review:

My favorite part/quote:

My favorite character:

Someone I know who would love this book:

Star rating:	Tears shed:	Spice meter:
☆ ☆ ☆ ☆ ☆	◊ ◊ ◊ ◊ ◊	🌶 🌶 🌶 🌶 🌶

BOOK TITLE:
AUTHOR:

My review:

_____

_____

_____

_____

_____

_____

My favorite part/quote:

_____

_____

_____

_____

My favorite character:

_____

Someone I know who would love this book:

_____

Star rating: Tears shed: Spice meter:
☆ ☆ ☆ ☆ ☆   ◊ ◊ ◊ ◊ ◊   🌶 🌶 🌶 🌶 🌶

BOOK TITLE:
AUTHOR:

My review:

_____

_____

_____

_____

_____

_____

My favorite part/quote:

_____

_____

_____

_____

My favorite character:

_____

Someone I know who would love this book:

_____

Star rating:	Tears shed:	Spice meter:
☆ ☆ ☆ ☆ ☆	◇ ◇ ◇ ◇ ◇	🌶 🌶 🌶 🌶 🌶

BOOK TITLE:
AUTHOR:

My review:

_____

_____

_____

_____

_____

_____

My favorite part/quote:

_____

_____

_____

_____

My favorite character:

_____

Someone I know who would love this book:

_____

Star rating:	*Tears shed:*	*Spice meter:*
☆ ☆ ☆ ☆ ☆	◊ ◊ ◊ ◊ ◊	🌶 🌶 🌶 🌶 🌶

BOOK TITLE:
AUTHOR:

My review:

My favorite part/quote:

My favorite character:

Someone I know who would love this book:

Star rating:
☆ ☆ ☆ ☆ ☆

Tears shed:
◌ ◌ ◌ ◌ ◌

Spice meter:
🌶 🌶 🌶 🌶 🌶

BOOK TITLE:
AUTHOR:

My review:

_____

_____

_____

_____

_____

_____

My favorite part/quote:

_____

_____

_____

_____

My favorite character:

_____

Someone I know who would love this book:

_____

Star rating:
☆ ☆ ☆ ☆ ☆

Tears shed:
◊ ◊ ◊ ◊ ◊

Spice meter:
🌶 🌶 🌶 🌶 🌶

BOOK TITLE:
AUTHOR:

My review:

_____

_____

_____

_____

_____

My favorite part/quote:

_____

_____

_____

_____

My favorite character:

_____

Someone I know who would love this book:

_____

Star rating:	Tears shed:	Spice meter:
☆☆☆☆☆	○○○○○	🌶🌶🌶🌶🌶

BOOK TITLE:
AUTHOR:

My review:

_____

_____

_____

_____

_____

_____

My favorite part/quote:

_____

_____

_____

_____

My favorite character:

_____

Someone I know who would love this book:

_____

Star rating:	*Tears shed:*	*Spice meter:*
☆ ☆ ☆ ☆ ☆	◊ ◊ ◊ ◊ ◊	♪ ♪ ♪ ♪ ♪

BOOK TITLE:
AUTHOR:

My review:

My favorite part/quote:

My favorite character:

Someone I know who would love this book:

Star rating:	Tears shed:	Spice meter:
☆☆☆☆☆	◇◇◇◇◇	🌶🌶🌶🌶🌶

BOOK TITLE:
AUTHOR:

My review:

_____
_____
_____
_____
_____
_____

My favorite part/quote:

_____
_____
_____
_____

My favorite character:

_____

Someone I know who would love this book:

_____

Star rating:	Tears shed:	Spice meter:
☆ ☆ ☆ ☆ ☆	○ ○ ○ ○ ○	🌶 🌶 🌶 🌶 🌶

BOOK TITLE:
AUTHOR:

My review:

My favorite part/quote:

My favorite character:

Someone I know who would love this book:

Star rating:	Tears shed:	Spice meter:
☆☆☆☆☆	◊◊◊◊◊	🌶🌶🌶🌶🌶

BOOK TITLE:
AUTHOR:

My review:

_____
_____
_____
_____
_____
_____

My favorite part/quote:

_____
_____
_____
_____

My favorite character:

_____

Someone I know who would love this book:

_____

| Star rating: | Tears shed: | Spice meter: |
| ☆ ☆ ☆ ☆ ☆ | ◌ ◌ ◌ ◌ ◌ | 🌶 🌶 🌶 🌶 🌶 |

BOOK TITLE:
AUTHOR:

My review:

_____

_____

_____

_____

_____

_____

My favorite part/quote:

_____

_____

_____

_____

My favorite character:

_____

Someone I know who would love this book:

_____

Star rating:	Tears shed:	Spice meter:
☆ ☆ ☆ ☆ ☆	◯ ◯ ◯ ◯ ◯	🌶 🌶 🌶 🌶 🌶

BOOK TITLE:
AUTHOR:

My review:

_____
_____
_____
_____
_____
_____

My favorite part/quote:

_____
_____
_____
_____

My favorite character:

_____

Someone I know who would love this book:

_____

| Star rating: | Tears shed: | Spice meter: |
| ☆☆☆☆☆ | ○○○○○ | 🌶🌶🌶🌶🌶 |

BOOK TITLE:
AUTHOR:

My review:

_____
_____
_____
_____
_____
_____

My favorite part/quote:

_____
_____
_____
_____

My favorite character:

_____

Someone I know who would love this book:

_____

Star rating:	*Tears shed:*	*Spice meter:*
☆ ☆ ☆ ☆ ☆	◊ ◊ ◊ ◊ ◊	🌶 🌶 🌶 🌶 🌶

BOOK TITLE:
AUTHOR:

My review:

_____

_____

_____

_____

_____

_____

My favorite part/quote:

_____

_____

_____

My favorite character:

_____

Someone I know who would love this book:

_____

Star rating:	Tears shed:	Spice meter:
☆☆☆☆☆	◊◊◊◊◊	🌶🌶🌶🌶🌶

BOOK TITLE:
AUTHOR:

My review:

My favorite part/quote:

My favorite character:

Someone I know who would love this book:

Star rating:	Tears shed:	Spice meter:
☆ ☆ ☆ ☆ ☆	◊ ◊ ◊ ◊ ◊	🌶 🌶 🌶 🌶 🌶

BOOK TITLE:
AUTHOR:

My review:

_____

_____

_____

_____

_____

_____

My favorite part/quote:

_____

_____

_____

_____

My favorite character:

_____

Someone I know who would love this book:

_____

Star rating:	Tears shed:	Spice meter:
☆ ☆ ☆ ☆ ☆	◊ ◊ ◊ ◊ ◊	🌶 🌶 🌶 🌶 🌶

BOOK TITLE:

AUTHOR:

My review:

_____

_____

_____

_____

_____

_____

My favorite part/quote:

_____

_____

_____

_____

My favorite character:

_____

Someone I know who would love this book:

_____

Star rating:	Tears shed:	Spice meter:
☆ ☆ ☆ ☆ ☆	◊ ◊ ◊ ◊ ◊	🌶 🌶 🌶 🌶 🌶

BOOK TITLE:
AUTHOR:

My review:

_____

_____

_____

_____

_____

_____

My favorite part/quote:

_____

_____

_____

_____

My favorite character:

_____

Someone I know who would love this book:

_____

Star rating:	Tears shed:	Spice meter:
☆☆☆☆☆	◊◊◊◊◊	🌶🌶🌶🌶🌶

BOOK TITLE:
AUTHOR:

My review:

My favorite part/quote:

My favorite character:

Someone I know who would love this book:

Star rating:
☆☆☆☆☆

Tears shed:
◊ ◊ ◊ ◊ ◊

Spice meter:
🌶 🌶 🌶 🌶 🌶

BOOK TITLE:
AUTHOR:

My review:

_____
_____
_____
_____
_____
_____

My favorite part/quote:

_____
_____
_____
_____

My favorite character:

_____

Someone I know who would love this book:

_____

| Star rating: | Tears shed: | Spice meter: |
| ☆ ☆ ☆ ☆ ☆ | ◊ ◊ ◊ ◊ ◊ | 🌶 🌶 🌶 🌶 🌶 |

BOOK TITLE:
AUTHOR:

My review:

My favorite part/quote:

My favorite character:

Someone I know who would love this book:

Star rating:	Tears shed:	Spice meter:
☆☆☆☆☆	◊◊◊◊◊	🌶🌶🌶🌶🌶

BOOK TITLE:
AUTHOR:

My review:

_____

_____

_____

_____

_____

_____

My favorite part/quote:

_____

_____

_____

My favorite character:

_____

Someone I know who would love this book:

_____

Star rating: Tears shed: Spice meter:
☆ ☆ ☆ ☆ ☆   ◇ ◇ ◇ ◇ ◇   🌶 🌶 🌶 🌶 🌶

BOOK TITLE:
AUTHOR:

My review:

_____
_____
_____
_____
_____
_____

My favorite part/quote:

_____
_____
_____
_____

My favorite character:

_____

Someone I know who would love this book:

_____

| Star rating: | Tears shed: | Spice meter: |
| ☆ ☆ ☆ ☆ ☆ | ◊ ◊ ◊ ◊ ◊ | 🌶 🌶 🌶 🌶 🌶 |

BOOK TITLE:
AUTHOR:

My review:

My favorite part/quote:

My favorite character:

Someone I know who would love this book:

Star rating: ☆☆☆☆☆ Tears shed: ○○○○○ Spice meter: 🌶🌶🌶🌶🌶

BOOK TITLE:
AUTHOR:

My review:

_____
_____
_____
_____
_____
_____

My favorite part/quote:

_____
_____
_____
_____

My favorite character:

_____

Someone I know who would love this book:

_____

Star rating:	Tears shed:	Spice meter:
☆ ☆ ☆ ☆ ☆	◊ ◊ ◊ ◊ ◊	🌶 🌶 🌶 🌶 🌶

BOOK TITLE:
AUTHOR:

My review:

_____
_____
_____
_____
_____
_____

My favorite part/quote:

_____
_____
_____
_____

My favorite character:

_____

Someone I know who would love this book:

_____

| *Star rating:* | *Tears shed:* | *Spice meter:* |
| ☆ ☆ ☆ ☆ ☆ | ◊ ◊ ◊ ◊ ◊ | 🌶 🌶 🌶 🌶 🌶 |

BOOK TITLE:
AUTHOR:

My review:

My favorite part/quote:

My favorite character:

Someone I know who would love this book:

Star rating:	Tears shed:	Spice meter:
☆☆☆☆☆	◊◊◊◊◊	🌶🌶🌶🌶🌶

BOOK TITLE:
AUTHOR:

My review:

_____
_____
_____
_____
_____
_____

My favorite part/quote:

_____
_____
_____
_____

My favorite character:

_____

Someone I know who would love this book:

_____

Star rating:	Tears shed:	Spice meter:
☆☆☆☆☆	◇◇◇◇◇	🌶🌶🌶🌶🌶

BOOK TITLE:
AUTHOR:

My review:

_____

_____

_____

_____

_____

_____

My favorite part/quote:

_____

_____

_____

_____

My favorite character:

_____

Someone I know who would love this book:

_____

Star rating:	Tears shed:	Spice meter:
☆☆☆☆☆	◊◊◊◊◊	🌶🌶🌶🌶🌶

BOOK TITLE:
AUTHOR:

My review:

_____
_____
_____
_____
_____
_____

My favorite part/quote:

_____
_____
_____

My favorite character:

_____

Someone I know who would love this book:

_____

Star rating:
☆ ☆ ☆ ☆ ☆

Tears shed:
◊ ◊ ◊ ◊ ◊

Spice meter:
🌶 🌶 🌶 🌶 🌶

BOOK TITLE:
AUTHOR:

My review:

_____
_____
_____
_____
_____

My favorite part/quote:

_____
_____
_____
_____

My favorite character:

_____

Someone I know who would love this book:

_____

Star rating:	Tears shed:	Spice meter:
☆ ☆ ☆ ☆ ☆	◊ ◊ ◊ ◊ ◊	🌶 🌶 🌶 🌶 🌶

BOOK TITLE:
AUTHOR:

My review:

_____
_____
_____
_____
_____
_____

My favorite part/quote:

_____
_____
_____

My favorite character:

_____

Someone I know who would love this book:

_____

Star rating:	*Tears shed:*	*Spice meter:*
☆ ☆ ☆ ☆ ☆	◌ ◌ ◌ ◌ ◌	🌶 🌶 🌶 🌶 🌶

BOOK TITLE:
AUTHOR:

My review:

My favorite part/quote:

My favorite character:

Someone I know who would love this book:

Star rating:	Tears shed:	Spice meter:
☆☆☆☆☆	◊◊◊◊◊	🌶🌶🌶🌶🌶

BOOK TITLE:
AUTHOR:

My review:

My favorite part/quote:

My favorite character:

Someone I know who would love this book:

Star rating:
☆☆☆☆☆

Tears shed:
◇◇◇◇◇

Spice meter:
🌶🌶🌶🌶🌶

BOOK TITLE:
AUTHOR:

My review:

My favorite part/quote:

My favorite character:

Someone I know who would love this book:

Star rating:	Tears shed:	Spice meter:
☆ ☆ ☆ ☆ ☆	◊ ◊ ◊ ◊ ◊	🌶 🌶 🌶 🌶 🌶

BOOK TITLE:
AUTHOR:

My review:

_____

_____

_____

_____

_____

_____

My favorite part/quote:

_____

_____

_____

My favorite character:

_____

Someone I know who would love this book:

_____

Star rating:	Tears shed:	Spice meter:
☆ ☆ ☆ ☆ ☆	◊ ◊ ◊ ◊ ◊	🌶 🌶 🌶 🌶 🌶

BOOK TITLE:
AUTHOR:

My review:

My favorite part/quote:

My favorite character:

Someone I know who would love this book:

Star rating:
☆ ☆ ☆ ☆ ☆

Tears shed:
◊ ◊ ◊ ◊ ◊

Spice meter:
🌶 🌶 🌶 🌶 🌶

BOOK TITLE:
AUTHOR:

My review:

_____
_____
_____
_____
_____
_____

My favorite part/quote:

_____
_____
_____
_____

My favorite character:

_____

Someone I know who would love this book:

_____

| Star rating: | Tears shed: | Spice meter: |
| ☆☆☆☆☆ | ○○○○○ | 🌶🌶🌶🌶🌶 |

BOOK TITLE:
AUTHOR:

My review:

My favorite part/quote:

My favorite character:

Someone I know who would love this book:

Star rating: ☆☆☆☆☆   Tears shed: ○○○○○   Spice meter: 🌶🌶🌶🌶🌶

BOOK TITLE:
AUTHOR:

My review:

My favorite part/quote:

My favorite character:

Someone I know who would love this book:

Star rating: ☆☆☆☆☆   Tears shed: ◊◊◊◊◊   Spice meter: 🌶🌶🌶🌶🌶

BOOK TITLE:
AUTHOR:

My review:

_____
_____
_____
_____
_____
_____

My favorite part/quote:

_____
_____
_____
_____

My favorite character:

_____

Someone I know who would love this book:

_____

| Star rating: | Tears shed: | Spice meter: |
| ☆☆☆☆☆ | ◊ ◊ ◊ ◊ ◊ | 🌶 🌶 🌶 🌶 🌶 |

BOOK TITLE:
AUTHOR:

My review:

_____

_____

_____

_____

_____

_____

My favorite part/quote:

_____

_____

_____

_____

My favorite character:

_____

Someone I know who would love this book:

_____

Star rating:
☆ ☆ ☆ ☆ ☆

Tears shed:
◊ ◊ ◊ ◊ ◊

Spice meter:
🌶 🌶 🌶 🌶 🌶

BOOK TITLE:
AUTHOR:

My review:

_____
_____
_____
_____
_____
_____

My favorite part/quote:

_____
_____
_____
_____

My favorite character:

_____

Someone I know who would love this book:

_____

Star rating: Tears shed: Spice meter:
☆ ☆ ☆ ☆ ☆   ◌ ◌ ◌ ◌ ◌   🌶 🌶 🌶 🌶 🌶

BOOK TITLE:
AUTHOR:

My review:

_____
_____
_____
_____
_____
_____

My favorite part/quote:

_____
_____
_____
_____

My favorite character:

_____

Someone I know who would love this book:

_____

| Star rating: | Tears shed: | Spice meter: |
| ☆☆☆☆☆ | ◇◇◇◇◇ | 🌶🌶🌶🌶🌶 |

BOOK TITLE:
AUTHOR:

My review:

My favorite part/quote:

My favorite character:

Someone I know who would love this book:

Star rating:	Tears shed:	Spice meter:
☆ ☆ ☆ ☆ ☆	◌ ◌ ◌ ◌ ◌	🌶 🌶 🌶 🌶 🌶

BOOK TITLE:
AUTHOR:

My review:

_____

_____

_____

_____

_____

_____

My favorite part/quote:

_____

_____

_____

_____

My favorite character:

_____

Someone I know who would love this book:

_____

| *Star rating:* | *Tears shed:* | *Spice meter:* |
| ☆ ☆ ☆ ☆ ☆ | ◇ ◇ ◇ ◇ ◇ | 🌶 🌶 🌶 🌶 🌶 |

BOOK TITLE:
AUTHOR:

My review:

My favorite part/quote:

My favorite character:

Someone I know who would love this book:

Star rating:	Tears shed:	Spice meter:
☆☆☆☆☆	◌◌◌◌◌	🌶🌶🌶🌶🌶

BOOK TITLE:
AUTHOR:

My review:

_____

_____

_____

_____

_____

My favorite part/quote:

_____

_____

_____

My favorite character:

_____

Someone I know who would love this book:

_____

Star rating:
☆ ☆ ☆ ☆ ☆

Tears shed:
 ◊ ◊ ◊ ◊ ◊

Spice meter:

BOOK TITLE:
AUTHOR:

My review:

My favorite part/quote:

My favorite character:

Someone I know who would love this book:

Star rating:	Tears shed:	Spice meter:
☆ ☆ ☆ ☆ ☆	◊ ◊ ◊ ◊ ◊	🌶 🌶 🌶 🌶 🌶

BOOK TITLE:
AUTHOR:

My review:

_____
_____
_____
_____
_____
_____

My favorite part/quote:

_____
_____
_____
_____

My favorite character:

_____

Someone I know who would love this book:

_____

Star rating:
☆ ☆ ☆ ☆ ☆

Tears shed:
◇ ◇ ◇ ◇ ◇

Spice meter:
🌶 🌶 🌶 🌶 🌶

BOOK TITLE:
AUTHOR:

My review:

_____
_____
_____
_____
_____
_____

My favorite part/quote:

_____
_____
_____
_____

My favorite character:

_____

Someone I know who would love this book:

_____

Star rating:	Tears shed:	Spice meter:
☆☆☆☆☆	◌◌◌◌◌	🌶🌶🌶🌶🌶

BOOK TITLE:
AUTHOR:

My review:

_____
_____
_____
_____
_____
_____

My favorite part/quote:

_____
_____
_____
_____

My favorite character:

_____

Someone I know who would love this book:

_____

| Star rating: | Tears shed: | Spice meter: |
| ☆☆☆☆☆ | ◇◇◇◇◇ | 🌶🌶🌶🌶🌶 |

BOOK TITLE:
AUTHOR:

My review:

_____
_____
_____
_____
_____
_____

My favorite part/quote:

_____
_____
_____

My favorite character:

_____

Someone I know who would love this book:

_____

Star rating:	Tears shed:	Spice meter:
☆☆☆☆☆	◌◌◌◌◌	🌶🌶🌶🌶🌶

BOOK TITLE:
AUTHOR:

My review:

My favorite part/quote:

My favorite character:

Someone I know who would love this book:

Star rating:
☆ ☆ ☆ ☆ ☆

Tears shed:
◇ ◇ ◇ ◇ ◇

Spice meter:
🌶 🌶 🌶 🌶 🌶

BOOK TITLE:
AUTHOR:

My review:

My favorite part/quote:

My favorite character:

Someone I know who would love this book:

Star rating:	Tears shed:	Spice meter:
☆☆☆☆☆	◌◌◌◌◌	🌶🌶🌶🌶🌶

BOOK TITLE:
AUTHOR:

My review:

_____
_____
_____
_____
_____
_____

My favorite part/quote:

_____
_____
_____
_____

My favorite character:

_____

Someone I know who would love this book:

_____

Star rating: Tears shed: Spice meter:
☆ ☆ ☆ ☆ ☆   ◊ ◊ ◊ ◊ ◊   🌶 🌶 🌶 🌶 🌶

BOOK TITLE:
AUTHOR:

My review:

My favorite part/quote:

My favorite character:

Someone I know who would love this book:

Star rating:	Tears shed:	Spice meter:
☆ ☆ ☆ ☆ ☆	◊ ◊ ◊ ◊ ◊	🌶 🌶 🌶 🌶 🌶

BOOK TITLE:
AUTHOR:

My review:

_____

_____

_____

_____

_____

_____

My favorite part/quote:

_____

_____

_____

_____

My favorite character:

_____

Someone I know who would love this book:

_____

| *Star rating:* | *Tears shed:* | *Spice meter:* |
| ☆☆☆☆☆ | ◊◊◊◊◊ | 🌶🌶🌶🌶🌶 |

BOOK TITLE:
AUTHOR:

My review:

_____

_____

_____

_____

_____

My favorite part/quote:

_____

_____

_____

_____

My favorite character:

_____

Someone I know who would love this book:

_____

Star rating:	Tears shed:	Spice meter:
☆☆☆☆☆	◊ ◊ ◊ ◊ ◊	🌶 🌶 🌶 🌶 🌶

BOOK TITLE:
AUTHOR:

My review:

_____

_____

_____

_____

_____

_____

My favorite part/quote:

_____

_____

_____

_____

My favorite character:

_____

Someone I know who would love this book:

_____

Star rating:	*Tears shed:*	*Spice meter:*
☆ ☆ ☆ ☆ ☆	◊ ◊ ◊ ◊ ◊	🌶 🌶 🌶 🌶 🌶

BOOK TITLE:
AUTHOR:

My review:

_____
_____
_____
_____
_____
_____

My favorite part/quote:

_____
_____
_____
_____

My favorite character:

_____

Someone I know who would love this book:

_____

Star rating:	Tears shed:	Spice meter:
☆ ☆ ☆ ☆ ☆	◇ ◇ ◇ ◇ ◇	🌶 🌶 🌶 🌶 🌶

BOOK TITLE:
AUTHOR:

My review:

_____
_____
_____
_____
_____
_____

My favorite part/quote:

_____
_____
_____
_____

My favorite character:

_____

Someone I know who would love this book:

_____

Star rating:	Tears shed:	Spice meter:
☆ ☆ ☆ ☆ ☆	◊ ◊ ◊ ◊ ◊	🌶 🌶 🌶 🌶 🌶

BOOK TITLE:
AUTHOR:

My review:

My favorite part/quote:

My favorite character:

Someone I know who would love this book:

Star rating:	Tears shed:	Spice meter:
☆ ☆ ☆ ☆ ☆	◊ ◊ ◊ ◊ ◊	🌶 🌶 🌶 🌶 🌶

BOOK TITLE:
AUTHOR:

My review:

_____
_____
_____
_____
_____
_____

My favorite part/quote:

_____
_____
_____
_____

My favorite character:

_____

Someone I know who would love this book:

_____

| Star rating: | Tears shed: | Spice meter: |
| ☆☆☆☆☆ | ◌◌◌◌◌ | 🌶🌶🌶🌶🌶 |

BOOK TITLE:
AUTHOR:

My review:

My favorite part/quote:

My favorite character:

Someone I know who would love this book:

Star rating:	Tears shed:	Spice meter:
☆☆☆☆☆	◊◊◊◊◊	🌶🌶🌶🌶🌶

BOOK TITLE:
AUTHOR:

My review:

_____

_____

_____

_____

_____

_____

My favorite part/quote:

_____

_____

_____

_____

My favorite character:

_____

Someone I know who would love this book:

_____

Star rating:
☆ ☆ ☆ ☆ ☆

Tears shed:
◊ ◊ ◊ ◊ ◊

Spice meter:
🌶 🌶 🌶 🌶 🌶

BOOK TITLE:
AUTHOR:

My review:

_____
_____
_____
_____
_____
_____

My favorite part/quote:

_____
_____
_____
_____

My favorite character:

_____

Someone I know who would love this book:

_____

Star rating:
☆ ☆ ☆ ☆ ☆

Tears shed:
◊ ◊ ◊ ◊ ◊

Spice meter:
🌶 🌶 🌶 🌶 🌶

BOOK TITLE:
AUTHOR:

My review:

_____
_____
_____
_____
_____
_____

My favorite part/quote:

_____
_____
_____
_____

My favorite character:

_____

Someone I know who would love this book:

_____

Star rating:	Tears shed:	Spice meter:
☆ ☆ ☆ ☆ ☆	◊ ◊ ◊ ◊ ◊	🌶 🌶 🌶 🌶 🌶

BOOK TITLE:
AUTHOR:

My review:

_____

_____

_____

_____

_____

_____

My favorite part/quote:

_____

_____

_____

_____

My favorite character:

_____

Someone I know who would love this book:

_____

Star rating:	Tears shed:	Spice meter:
☆ ☆ ☆ ☆ ☆	◊ ◊ ◊ ◊ ◊	🌶 🌶 🌶 🌶 🌶

BOOK TITLE:
AUTHOR:

My review:

_____
_____
_____
_____
_____
_____
_____

My favorite part/quote:

_____
_____
_____
_____

My favorite character:

_____

Someone I know who would love this book:

_____

Star rating:
☆ ☆ ☆ ☆ ☆

Tears shed:
◊ ◊ ◊ ◊ ◊

Spice meter:
🌶 🌶 🌶 🌶 🌶

BOOK TITLE:
AUTHOR:

My review:

_____
_____
_____
_____
_____

My favorite part/quote:

_____
_____
_____
_____

My favorite character:

_____

Someone I know who would love this book:

_____

| Star rating: | Tears shed: | Spice meter: |
| ☆☆☆☆☆ | ◊◊◊◊◊ | 🌶🌶🌶🌶🌶 |

BOOK TITLE:
AUTHOR:

My review:

_____
_____
_____
_____
_____
_____

My favorite part/quote:

_____
_____
_____
_____

My favorite character:

_____

Someone I know who would love this book:

_____

Star rating:	Tears shed:	Spice meter:
☆ ☆ ☆ ☆ ☆	◌ ◌ ◌ ◌ ◌	🌶 🌶 🌶 🌶 🌶

BOOK TITLE:
AUTHOR:

My review:

_____

_____

_____

_____

_____

My favorite part/quote:

_____

_____

_____

_____

My favorite character:

_____

Someone I know who would love this book:

_____

Star rating:	Tears shed:	Spice meter:
☆☆☆☆☆	◊◊◊◊◊	🌶🌶🌶🌶🌶

BOOK TITLE:
AUTHOR:

My review:

_____
_____
_____
_____
_____
_____

My favorite part/quote:

_____
_____
_____

My favorite character:

_____

Someone I know who would love this book:

_____

Star rating:	Tears shed:	Spice meter:
☆☆☆☆☆	◊◊◊◊◊	🌶🌶🌶🌶🌶

BOOK TITLE:
AUTHOR:

My review:

_____
_____
_____
_____
_____
_____

My favorite part/quote:

_____
_____
_____
_____

My favorite character:

_____

Someone I know who would love this book:

_____

| Star rating: | Tears shed: | Spice meter: |
| ☆ ☆ ☆ ☆ ☆ | ⬭ ⬭ ⬭ ⬭ ⬭ | 🌶 🌶 🌶 🌶 🌶 |

BOOK TITLE:
AUTHOR:

My review:

_____

_____

_____

_____

_____

_____

My favorite part/quote:

_____

_____

_____

_____

My favorite character:

_____

Someone I know who would love this book:

_____

| Star rating: | Tears shed: | Spice meter: |
| ☆☆☆☆☆ | ◊◊◊◊◊ | 🌶🌶🌶🌶🌶 |

BOOK TITLE:
AUTHOR:

My review:

My favorite part/quote:

My favorite character:

Someone I know who would love this book:

Star rating:	Tears shed:	Spice meter:
☆☆☆☆☆	◊◊◊◊◊	🌶🌶🌶🌶🌶

BOOK TITLE:
AUTHOR:

My review:

_____

_____

_____

_____

_____

_____

My favorite part/quote:

_____

_____

_____

_____

My favorite character:

_____

Someone I know who would love this book:

_____

| *Star rating:* | *Tears shed:* | *Spice meter:* |
| ☆☆☆☆☆ | ◇◇◇◇◇ | 🌶🌶🌶🌶🌶 |

MY BOOKTOK
Year in Review

Books that destroyed me:

1. _____

2. _____

3. _____

Books I would give anything to read again for the first time:

1. _____

2. _____

3. _____

Books that are overrated:

1. _____

2. _____

3. _____

Books with gasp-worthy endings:

1. _____

2. _____

3. _____

Books with just the right spice:

1. _____

2. _____

3. _____

Characters I fell in love with:

1. _____

2. _____

3. _____

Characters I'm most like:

1. _____

2. _____

3. _____

Books I wish had a sequel:

1. _____

2. _____

3. _____

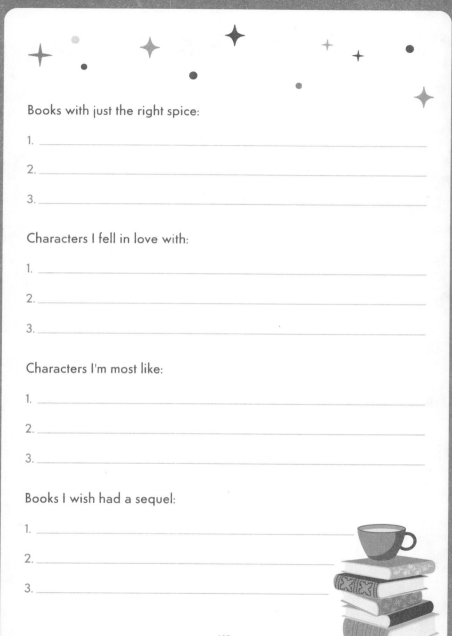

MY BOOKTOK LOG

NUMBER OF BOOKS I'VE READ THIS YEAR:

My Top 10 BookTok Books of

_____
YEAR

1. _____

2. _____

3. _____

4. _____

5. _____

6. _____

7. _____

8. _____

9. _____

10. _____